Scott Foresman - Addison Wesley

Teacher's Toolkit

Grade 3

Scott Foresman - Addison Wesley

Editorial Offices: Menlo Park, California • Glenview, Illinois
Sales Offices: Reading, Massachusetts • Atlanta, Georgia • Glenview, Illinois
Carrollton, Texas • Menlo Park, California

http://www.sf.aw.com

Overview

Teacher's Toolkit provides a collection of masters, transparencies, and management resources to assist with classroom management.

Classroom management resources provide suggestions for incorporating language skills into mathematics, providing cooperative learning experiences, and utilizing additional teaching strategies. Copies of the one-page lesson plan can assist in lesson preparation. A complete vocabulary list of all the words introduced in the *Student's Edition* is included, as is the entire student literature bibliography listed in the *Teacher's Edition.*

Teaching Tool Transparencies include tools, gameboards, maps, and other materials referred to in the *Teacher's Edition.* Many of the sheets that accompany these transparencies can be copied and used by students to facilitate learning.

ISBN 0–201–31387-1

Copyright © Addison Wesley Longman, Inc.

All rights reserved.

Printed in the United States of America

5 6 7 8 9 10 – VSI – 02 01 00 99 98

Table of Contents

Using Classroom Management Resources

There are several types of management resources available in the *Teacher's Toolkit*. Each resource offers options for you to use in meeting students' diversified needs.

English Language Development

This section provides general strategies that a teacher can use to help students who are not yet proficient in the English language.

Strategies for Teaching Vocabulary

This section provides guidance for effective vocabulary instruction and suggests vocabulary activities that use a variety of approaches and materials.

Cooperative Learning

This section provides the teacher with ways to maximize student learning when structuring activities that involve students working together as a team.

Additional Teaching Strategies

This section explores different teaching strategies that a teacher can use while working with students who are visually impaired, learning disabled, and so on.

Lesson Planner

This page can be used by the teacher to plan what he or she will do the next day in class. This tool can be prepared in advance and becomes invaluable to a substitute teacher when the teacher is absent.

Vocabulary Lists

The vocabulary list is compiled by chapter. In Kindergarten, each vocabulary word is keyed to the lesson where it is used. In grades 1–8, each word is keyed to the page number where it is introduced.

Literature Bibliography

The two-page section provides a list of articles and books. The books are compiled by chapter and are related to the math content.

Classroom Management Resources

English Language Development

Students learning English as a second language (ESL) may need more time to make connections between concepts and mathematical language than other students. Most of these students are capable of performing work at their grade level and want to succeed in school, but their difficulty in communicating and the resulting problems often overwhelms and frustrates them.

Teachers who want to encourage growth and learning for these students are encouraged to draw upon what students already know and provide many opportunities for students to listen, speak, and write within these parameters. It is important that teachers use new terms frequently and encourage students to define mathematical terms in their own words.

Here are some general strategies that the teacher can use to help ESL students.

Provide a positive learning environment.

Make sure that students are comfortable enough to risk speaking and communicating in English without feeling ashamed if they are not always on target with the "correct" word or phrase. Emphasize communication, not English word and sentence structure.

Use manipulatives.

Manipulatives, such as place-value blocks, can be used to model mathematical concepts. Encourage students to describe the models using their own words. Other concrete approaches, such as pantomime and role-playing, may also be used when presenting new content.

Encourage both observation and participation.

Although one needs to encourage observation and participation, the teacher needs to be aware that the beginning language learner often goes through a period of limited participation. This is a learning period and does not indicate a lack of interest unless it continues for a long period of time. Therefore, the teacher should not force participation but wait until the student is comfortable enough to participate willingly in discussions. One way to elicit responses from these students is to ask questions that enable students to respond in nonverbal ways as well as in verbal ways. Thus, students do not feel threatened by their lack of command of the English language.

Encourage students to create visual displays.

It is especially important to encourage students to create visual displays when answering questions and when illustrating mathematical concepts. Have the students label the pictures with the appropriate symbols and words. This reinforces both the mathematical concept and the English terms used in relation with the concept.

Emphasize other cultures.

Create opportunities for students to use examples of mathematics from other cultures. Encourage students to make up their own problems that are rooted in familiar cultural perspectives.

Avoid rote or repetitive assignments.

Use assignments that stimulate students' thinking as they build their language skills. Encourage students to think critically and provide many activities that encourage creativity. It is especially important that teachers do not isolate students through excessive special assignments.

Emphasize cooperative learning.

Provide cooperative learning activities. Depending on the activities involved, teachers may want to team ESL students with others of similar backgrounds to generate a sense of camaraderie as both pursue a common goal. For other activities, teachers may wish to team ESL students with English-proficient students to further develop students' language skills.

At other times, teachers may want to use small group activities. Students often feel less pressured when working in a group and are more likely to take risks in this type of situation. Small group activities provide an atmosphere that fosters a natural situation in which students acquire language skills as well as building mathematical concepts.

Use paraphrasing and synonyms.

Build in reinforcement of English words with repetition, paraphrasing, and the use of synonyms. When speaking, use shorter sentences and repeat the concept in several different ways. This will reduce the pressure of using and understanding more complex sentence construction. During question-and-answer periods, allow students extra time to decode English words and make the appropriate calculations before they respond.

Explore multiple meanings of words.

When using vocabulary words that have more than one meaning, take time to explore each meaning and how it applies to the current situation. For example, a word such as *operation* can mean something that happens in a hospital or something one does with numbers. Elicit from students which meaning is appropriate to use in the current situation.

Accept all valid responses.

Accept a variety of responses as valid means of communication. For example, a student may choose to answer with gestures or make an attempt to act it out. Allowing the use of body language as a response can help the ESL students clarify the concept. Reinforce the concept by summarizing the response in English.

For example, when a student responds to the question "What figure has 4 sides and 4 right angles?" by drawing a square, you may wish to point to the picture and say, "Yes, a square is one figure that has 4 sides and 4 right angles."

Provide positive feedback.

Always try to model correct language usage for students rather than constantly correcting students' grammatical errors.

Always praise a student when he or she achieves success. If a sentence is incomplete or contains grammatical errors but the concept is correct, reinforce the student's attempt by saying "That's right." and then repeating the sentence correctly.

Monitor students' progress.

Review students' work frequently. Adjust instruction as needed.

Provide materials for bilingual students.

It is important to have an abundance of dictionaries, glossaries, and visual materials for students to use in the classroom.

Additional tips for teaching ESL students that relate directly to the lesson can be found in the Teacher's Edition. *Teaching Tool Transparencies* keyed to specific lessons ensure that these students' needs can be met using materials developed specifically for this elementary program.

Strategies for Teaching Vocabulary

It is essential that students gain proficiency in the vocabulary presented in the context of each lesson. Whenever possible, you can use visual aids, diagrams or pictures, and concrete objects when introducing new vocabulary words to help students visualize the meaning of the new word. Give special emphasis to vocabulary that is confusing for students with language or reading difficulties.

Introducing math vocabulary

All students are first introduced to new math vocabulary as the teacher guides them through the initial teaching steps for a lesson. Students in grades 3–8 also have the vocabulary words and definitions listed under Vocabulary on the pupil page in the lesson where it appears, and each new word is highlighted in the actual lesson where it is first used. All vocabulary words used at your grade level are listed in the *Vocabulary Lists* in this section.

When introducing new vocabulary words, it is important to introduce only one word at a time. Write the word on the chalkboard. Then say the word aloud and have students repeat it. This procedure often helps students fix the word in their minds, although it does little to reinforce the meaning. To do this, teachers can provide a real-world example that illustrates the word and allows students to relate it to their own prior experiences.

Example: Suppose the teacher needs to introduce the word *fraction*.

1. Write some fractions on the chalkboard.

2. Point to the fractions on the chalkboard and say, "These are examples of some fractions. Fractions can name a part of a whole."

3. Have students repeat the word.

4. Create a real-world situation, such as cutting an orange in half, that illustrates the word. To reinforce the meaning of the word, bring a real orange to class and demonstrate.

5. Have students use clay to make pseudo oranges and cut each of them in half.

Introducing non-math vocabulary

An unfamiliar word may sometimes be used in the student text. If the meaning of such a word is not addressed by the teacher at the beginning of the lesson, the student may have difficulty in completing the assignment. The teacher may wish to use the pictures in the student book to reinforce the word and its meaning. If none are available, you may wish to bring some pictures to the classroom, draw a diagram, or have students act it out.

Example: Suppose the teacher needs to introduce the word *dinosaur*.

1. Hold up the picture or a model.

2. Point to the picture or model and say, "This is a dinosaur."

3. Have students repeat the word.

4. Use the word in several short sentences, such as "The dinosaur is a very large animal. The dinosaur lived long ago."

5. Hold up another picture or model of a dinosaur and ask the class to identify it.

6. Ask volunteers to use the word in a sentence.

7. Be positive and upbeat. Allow students many opportunities to communicate and use the new vocabulary.

Teaching and reinforcing vocabulary

Teaching and reinforcing vocabulary is as important as introducing the new words. A teacher can use various methods to reinforce vocabulary introduced in any math lesson.

Example: Suppose students have just been introduced to *regroup*.

1. Encourage students to write a definition for *regroup* in their journal.

2. Have them write a sentence using *regroup*.

3. Ask them to draw a picture or a diagram that visually represents the meaning of *regroup*. Encourage them to write *regroup* underneath the picture or diagram.

4. Encourage all students to write a short story that uses *regroup* correctly.

Activities you can use to enhance and reinforce vocabulary learning

Flashcards Encourage students to make flashcards for new vocabulary words by writing the word on one side of the card and its definition on the other. They can then use the cards as repetitive practice to reinforce the word and its meaning. This could be done individually or in pairs.

Bulletin board Make a bulletin board display of important vocabulary words and use pictures as well as descriptions to match the words.

Learning center Have students use a tape recorder in the center to tape new words and their meanings. They can practice using the words in sentences. Then have them play their recordings back and edit their sentences if necessary.

Set up matching cards in the center. Encourage students to match the correct meanings to the correct vocabulary word.

Encourage students to use manipulatives contained in the center to represent vocabulary words whenever possible. Also have students use concrete examples to model new vocabulary words wherever applicable.

Play act When possible, have students write a skit using vocabulary words. Then let them perform the skit before other groups or classes.

Games you can use to enhance and reinforce vocabulary learning

Password (Five players) Students need paper and pencil and a stopwatch to play this game. Choose one player as the word giver. Form two teams of two players. The word giver writes the word on two slips of paper and gives the slip to a member of each team. That member gives a one-word clue to his or her teammate, and the teammate tries to guess the word. If the word is guessed, the team receives 10 points. If it is not guessed, the other team takes its turn. If the word is guessed, the team receives 9 points. If it is not guessed, the first team gets another chance with the value for guessing the word dropping to 8 points. This process is repeated until one team guesses the word. Play until one team reaches a set number of points, such as 50.

Categories (Two or more players) One person names a category, such as addition. The next player must name something that relates to addition, such as plus. Play continues until a player is stumped or uses a word that has already been named. This game is good to use for non-math words as well and encourages students to retrieve words from memory that may not be commonly used.

Words that make up a dollar! (Any number of players) Each player needs paper and pencil to play this game. Calculators and dictionaries may be helpful but are not essential to a student's success. Write the alphabet on the chalkboard and include the numbers below beside the letters.

A, 1	B, 2	C, 3	D, 4	E, 5	F, 6	G, 7
H, 8	I, 9	J, 10	K, 11	L, 12	M, 13	N, 14
O, 15	P, 16	Q, 17	R, 18	S, 19	T, 20	U, 21
V, 22	W, 23	X, 24	Y, 25	Z, 26		

Encourage players to find words whose letters add up exactly to 100. You may wish to have students compile a classroom list of all the dollar words they are able to find.

Cooperative Learning

When students work cooperatively, they become motivated, enthusiastic learners. The benefits of cooperative learning include improved attitudes toward school, increased powers of retention, and greater sensitivity to the interest and needs of others. The basis of cooperative learning is positive interdependence; the approach goes beyond simply telling students to work in pairs or groups. Rather, cooperative learning is an experience through which students realize that they are united in a common endeavor; that they will succeed or fail as a team. Besides interdependence, cooperative learning fosters individual accountability—students understand that they are each responsible for learning the content of the lessons.

Forming an effective cooperative learning group involves more that just putting students together in small groups and giving them a problem to solve. The teacher must give careful attention to the needs of the students in order to elicit the most benefits from the process. The teacher can facilitate learning in cooperative groups by

- deciding whether to place students in random or heterogeneous groups.
- modeling appropriate social skills, such as ways to offer encouragement and help to another member of the group.
- rearranging the classroom so that students have ample space to work without distracting other groups.
- making sure that the students know what they are going to do, why they are going to do it, and how they are expected to work.

Choose lessons for cooperative learning activities that have many possible answers and allow students to choose from many different strategies when solving the problem. Be sure to allow adequate time for summarizing so that groups have an opportunity to share their solutions and questions. The resulting discussion can lead them to generalize from the specific problem by looking for patterns or relationships in the data.

How to Use Cooperative Learning Groups

Some teachers place students in groups to check math homework and reach a common solution to each problem. This approach works best when each student has completed the homework assignment.

Other teachers use small groups as a follow-up to whole-group instruction. Students in each group work on problems related to the lesson. By giving students an opportunity to apply newly-learned skills to a real-world situation, the teacher reinforces the learning that has taken place.

Yet other teachers use small groups as the way to develop the lesson itself. In this situation, the students, as a team, work through the problem or activity at their own pace and the group reaches a consensus on the answer or answers to the problem.

Developing Necessary Social Skills

Encourage students to develop the following social skills so that students can work together in a friendly fashion and focus on the problem at hand. The teacher may want to post these rules on the bulletin board so that students can easily refer to them.

Basic classroom rules
- Listen to what other have to say.
- Respect others and their ideas.
- Take your responsibilities seriously.
- Stick to the task at hand.

Actions of a cooperative group member
- Stays with the group, speaks quietly, and shares materials.
- Addresses others by name, looks at the person speaking, and encourages others to participate.
- Looks at the group's work and contributes ideas.
- Allows each person to respond before speaking again.

Actions of an effective group member
- Criticizes ideas without criticizing people.
- States the differences when there is a disagreement.
- Pulls together all the ideas into a single position.
- Asks others to verbalize how they would solve a problem or reach a decision.
- Asks people to explain their reasoning.
- Seeks elaboration by referring to other learning or knowledge.
- Builds on others' ideas.
- Listens to all ideas before reaching a conclusion.

How to Set Up a Cooperative Learning Group
Sometimes the teacher may need to assign roles to group members. Other times, the teacher may let students choose the roles they will play in solving the problem. These roles can include the following.

Reader: The reader reads the problem to the groups and makes sure every group member understands what he or she is to do. The reader makes sure that the group as a whole stays on task.

Materials manager: The materials manager gathers all the materials needed to complete the activity–paper, blocks, cubes, play money, graph paper, and so on. The manager is also responsible for cleaning up the work area and returning any unused materials.

Recorder: The recorder takes notes as the group completes the task or solves the problem. The recorder reviews his or her notes, and writes the answer or conclusions in a final form to be given to the reader or reporter.

Calculator: The calculator does the computation necessary to complete the task.

Checker: The checker checks the group's work or answers before turning over the work to the reporter or teacher.

Reporter: The reporter summarizes the group's work for the class or teacher and reports the answers and turns in the group's work to the teacher.

Every student should have the opportunity to play each role at different times during the year. You may want to prepare a set of posters that name and describe each role. Keep the posters visible during cooperative learning activities.

Additional Teaching Strategies

There are several teaching strategies the teacher can use when teaching mathematics. Some of these strategies are shown below. Often, strategies are combined or seem to overlap. For instance, the example given when using manipulatives and modeling also requires students to act out the problem to find a solution.

Encouraging student conversation

When students work in cooperative learning situations, encourage them to talk with each other about the tasks they perform. Encourage communication by asking students to describe what they are doing and explain why. A teacher may need to guide students in this type of interaction.

> **Example:** Suppose students are studying addition and subtraction of fractions.
>
> Ask Jorge to tell Linda why he removed a fraction piece from a model he made.

As the teacher listens to the conversations, he or she will be better able to decide what these students know and do not know. It is all right for students to disagree as long as they disagree about issues and do not let it escalate in disagreements between personalities. Disagreements that focus on issues can often open the door to higher-level thinking skills and provide ample opportunities for language use.

Using gestures

Using gestures can facilitate understanding. For example, when you are referring to an object, you may wish to focus students' attention on the object by holding it up for students to see or pointing to it in the classroom. Encourage students to use gestures whenever they have difficulty communicating in words.

> **Example 1:** Which of these basic facts are correct?
>
> Prepare several fact cards, some with incorrect answers. Have students respond with thumbs up when the fact shown is correct and with thumbs down when the fact shown is incorrect.

> **Example 2:** About how long is an inch? A foot? A yard?
>
> Ask students to practice holding their hands about 1 inch apart, 1 foot apart, and 1 yard apart. Then ask them to raise their hands when they think a minute has passed. These activities will help students gain a concrete understanding of units of measure.

Using manipulatives and modeling

The importance of using manipulatives when teaching concepts has been documented by extensive research. Manipulatives are tools that enable the teacher to provide multisensory learning experiences as the teacher models concepts. Manipulatives can also be used to reinforce concepts after they have been introduced. These learning experiences provide the foundation upon which students build as they move toward a greater level of abstraction.

Example 1: Carrie spends $4.15 and pays with a $5 bill. How much change will she receive?

Encourage students to use play money to count out the change Carrie will receive.

Example 2: Several cardboard triangles in different shapes are randomly mixed so that they may be turned or flipped. Have students match each triangle with another triangle in the group.

Be sure students understand that they may need to look for turned or flipped shapes in order to make all the matches.

Example 3: Give students exactly 100 counters of various colors and have them make a tally sheet showing how many of each color there are. Then find the percent of each color.

Let students work in pairs as they count and tally the counters. Encourage them to verbalize or write how they can find the percent of each color.

A teacher can use modeling to introduce a concept, such as regrouping sums. Often a student who is not English proficient will be able to understand quite well what is going on with the model. Having students model a concept can also be used to reinforce the concept once it is taught.

Example: Carmen and Jennie slide down one water slide. Eric slides down another water slide. How many students slide down the water slides?

Have students use counters to represent each student and pretend they are going down a slide. Slide two counters from an area designated as the top of the slide to an area designated as the bottom of the slide. Do the same thing with the other counter. Then ask students how many counters are at the bottom of the slide? Be sure they understand how their answer relates to the actual problem.

Acting out

Encourage students to act out a problem when confronted with a situation they cannot resolve. Acting out a problem actively involves students in the learning process. This method can be used to both introduce and reinforce concepts.

Example: May is sitting in the middle of a group of students on a park bench. There are 3 people on her right. How many people are sitting on the bench?

Encourage students to recreate the problem by having a student that represents May stand in a row. Then have 3 students stand on her right. Since she is in the middle, have another 3 students stand on her left. Then count the number of students in all. Another strategy students could use is Draw a Diagram.

Helping visually-impaired students learn

Different strategies need to be used to serve the needs of visually-impaired students. Type size on many of the learning materials may need to be larger so that students can focus on content without being distracted by his or her inability to see the words. For example, graphs need to be labeled clearly with large type so that students can read the scale on the graph. In other cases, objects can be made larger for the same reason.

Example: Is it likely or unlikely that you will draw a red marble?

Make sure that the jar is filled with marbles or other objects of distinctly different sizes and shapes to perform probability experiments.

Writing answers and problems

Encourage students to use their journal to write about what they learned in math that day as well as write answers to the Journal problems in the student book. Doing this helps students clarify their thinking and imprint in their mind the actual process they used to find the answer. Writing problems also builds students' language skills and demonstrates the underlying math understanding of the problem.

Example 1: Suppose you toss a number cube with sides labeled from 1 through 6 fifty times. Predict how many outcomes would be odd numbers. Explain your prediction.

Have students write the explanation in their journal and explain the process they used to decide upon their answers.

Example 2: Write a real-world problem that shows the joining of two sets of objects.

Encourage students to use complete sentences and correct terminology.

Lesson Plan

Teacher's Name _____   Date _____

Grade _____   M   T   W   Th   F

Lesson Objective _____

State/Local Objective _____

Lesson Resources

Blackline Masters

Practice Masters _____

Reteaching Masters _____

Enrichment Masters _____

Problem-Solving Masters _____

Technology Masters _____

Teacher Resources/Materials

Teaching Tool Transparencies _____

Problem of the Day Flipchart _____

Reading Strategies for Math _____

Lesson Enhancement Transparencies _____

Daily Transparencies _____

_____

Student Resources/Materials

Calculator _____   Grid paper _____   Colored paper _____

Manipulatives _____   _____

Assignment Guide

Basic _____

Average _____

Enriched _____

Assessment

_____

_____

_____

Using the Calendar Time Kit

Calendar _____   Graphs _____

Time _____   Temperature/Weather Map _____

Money _____   Number Line _____

Vocabulary Lists

Literature Bibliography (Grade 3)

For each book below, a short activity or math problem based on the literature selection appears in the Teacher's Edition on the A interleaf page of the lesson listed. Many of these titles are available through Cuisenaire/Dale Seymour Publications. Call 1-800-237-3142.

Lesson	Book Title / Author / Publisher
1-1	*20,000 Baseball Cards Under the Sea* / Jon Buller and Susan Schade / Random, 1991
1-8	"Uganda Near Kabalega Falls" from *Market* / Ted Lewin / Lothrop, 1996
2-4	*Zipping, Zapping, Zooming BATS* / Ann Earle / Harper, 1995
2-9	*Charlotte's Web* / E.B. White / HarperCollins, 1952
2-12	*The Grouchy Ladybug* / Eric Carle / HarperCollins, 1986
2-13	*Cloudy with a Chance of Meatballs* /Judi Barrett / Macmillan Children's Group, 1978
3-3	"Little Bits" from *You Read to Me, I'll Read to You* / John Ciardi / HarperCollins, 1987
3-7	*The 329th Friend* / Marjorie Weinman Sharmat / Macmillan, 1992
3-11	*Sideways Stories from Wayside School* / Louis Sachar / Camelot, 1985
4-4	*Once Upon Another* / Suse MacDonald & Bill Oakes / Dial, 1990
4-7	*Kid Power* / Susan Beth Pfeffer / Scholastic, 1991
4-15	*How to Make an Apple Pie and See the World* / Marjorie Priceman / Ramdom House, 1994
5-3	*One Hungry Monster A Counting Book in Rhyme* / Susan Heyboer O'Keefe / Little, 1989
5-6	*Two Ways to Count to Ten* / Ruby Dee / H. Holt, 1990
5-9	*The Cricket in Times Square* / George Selden / Dell, 1960
6-2	*The King's Chessboard* / David Birch / Dial, 1988
6-8	*Knock! Knock!* / Jackie Carter / Scholastic, 1993
7-1	*The Doorbell Rang* / Pat Hutchins / Greenwillow, 1986
7-4	"The Lamplighter" from *A Child's Garden of Verses* / Robert Louis Stevenson / Simon & Schuster, 1992
7-12	*Lucy and Tom's 1-2-3* / Shirley Hughes / Viking, 1987
8-1	*Round Buildings, Square Buildings, and Buildings that Wiggle Like a Fish* / Phillip M. Issacson / Knopf, 1990
8-2	"Shapes" from *A Light in the Attic* / Shel Silverstein / HarperCollins, 1981
8-4	*The Greedy Triangle* / Marilyn Burns / Scholastic, 1994
8-11	*Shapes* / Phillip Yenawine / The Museum of Modern Art / Delacorte, 1991

Lesson	Book Title / Author / Publisher
9-4	*Zipping, Zapping, Zooming BATS* / Ann Earle / Harper, 1995
9-6 and 9	*Counting on Frank* / Rod Clement / Garth Stevens, 1991
9-13	*A Remainder of One* / Elinor J. Pinczes / Houghton Mifflin, 1995
10-2	*Fractions Are Parts of Things* / J. Richard Dennis / Harper, 1972
10-6	*Wayside School is Falling Down* / Louis Sachar / Lothrop, 1989
10-14	*Melisande* / E. Nesbit / Harcourt Brace, 1989
11-4	*Kid Power* / Susan Beth Pfeffer / Scholastic, 1991
11-8	*Eloise* / Kay Thompson / Simon & Schuster, 1955
12-3	*Cranberries: Fruit of the Bogs* / Diane L. Burns / Carolrhoda Books, 1994
12-8	*One Hundred Hungry Ants* / Elinor J. Pinczes / Houghton Mifflin, 1993

Using Teaching Tool Transparencies

The *Teacher's Toolkit* offers a variety of transparencies. They are designed to be used with specific lessons and are keyed to those lessons in the *Teacher's Edition*. However, some *Teaching Tool Transparencies* can be incorporated into other areas of math instruction as well.

Example: At grades 3–8, teachers are encouraged to use the Guided Problem Solving transparencies any time they work through word problems with the class and not just when problem-solving lessons are presented in the student book.

The *Teaching Tool Transparencies* provide a way to accommodate group discussion while maintaining a hands-on approach to learning. They allow the teacher to illustrate math concepts at a concrete level.

Example: The teacher may model a math concept using a transparency while students imitate the model using manipulatives at their desks. Working at the concrete level along with the teacher helps build students' understanding of the concept being presented.

The sheets between the transparencies may be copied to provide students with identical tools, gameboards, or worksheets for independent or group work.

Teaching Tool Transparencies

Guided Problem Solving 1

Problem:

_____

_____

_____

_____

▬ Understand ▬

What do you know?
What do you need to find out?

▬ Plan ▬

What will you do?
What operation or strategy will you use?

Guided Problem Solving 2

━━ **Solve** ━━━━━━

How will you use your plan?
What is the answer?

━━ **Look Back** ━━━

Check your work.
Is your answer reasonable?

4-Digit Place-Value Charts

Thousands	Hundreds	Tens	Ones

Thousands	Hundreds	Tens	Ones

Number Lines

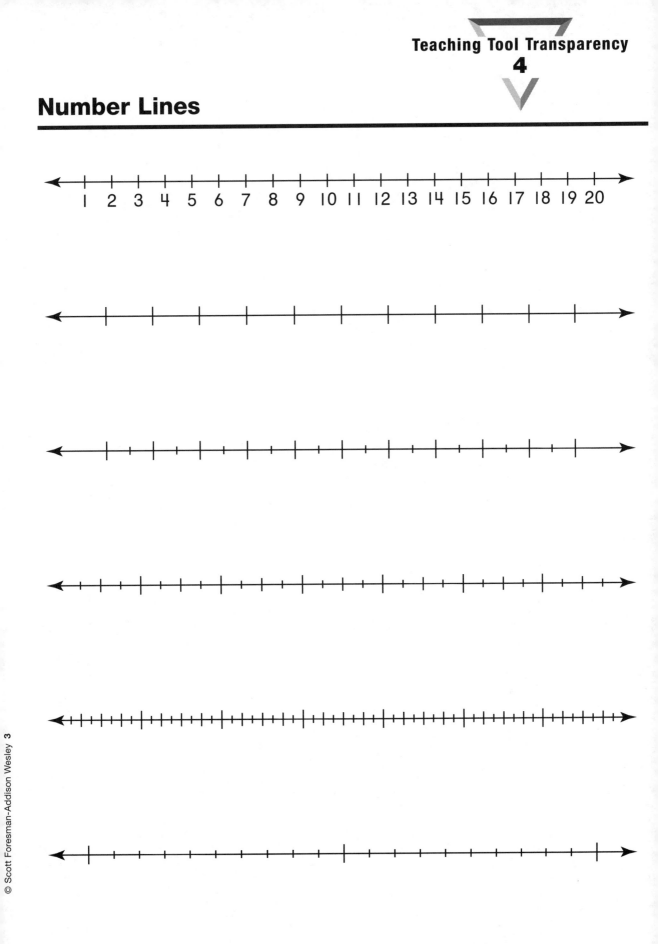

Centimeter Grid Paper

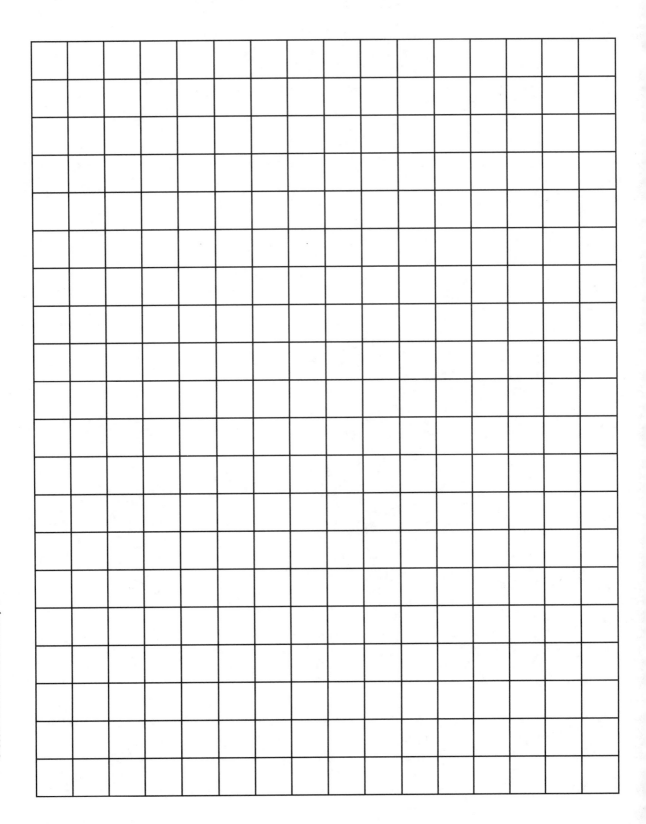

Geoboard Dot Paper

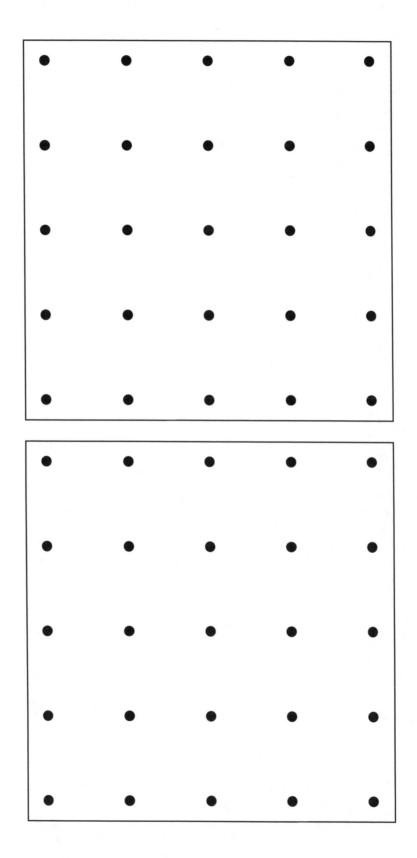

$\frac{1}{4}$-Inch Grid Paper

$\frac{1}{4}$-Inch Grid Paper

Hundred Chart

1	2	3	4	5	6	7	8	9	10
11	12	13	14	15	16	17	18	19	20
21	22	23	24	25	26	27	28	29	30
31	32	33	34	35	36	37	38	39	40
41	42	43	44	45	46	47	48	49	50
51	52	53	54	55	56	57	58	59	60
61	62	63	64	65	66	67	68	69	70
71	72	73	74	75	76	77	78	79	80
81	82	83	84	85	86	87	88	89	90
91	92	93	94	95	96	97	98	99	100

Addition/Multiplication Fact Table

	0	1	2	3	4	5	6	7	8	9
0										
1										
2										
3										
4										
5										
6										
7										
8										
9										

Tenths Grids

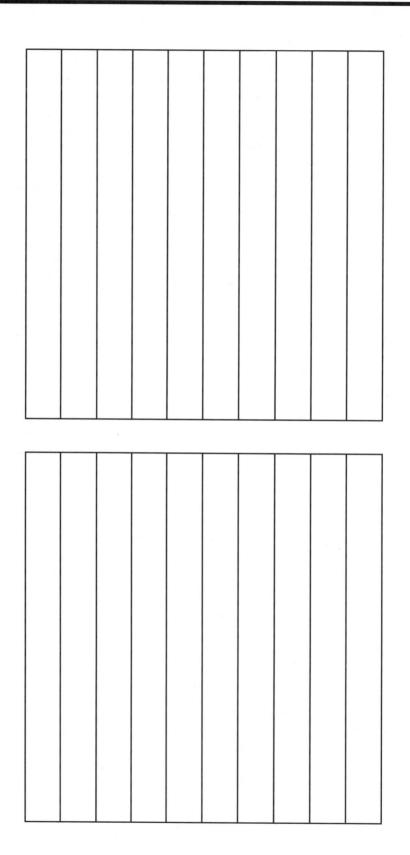

Hundredths Grids

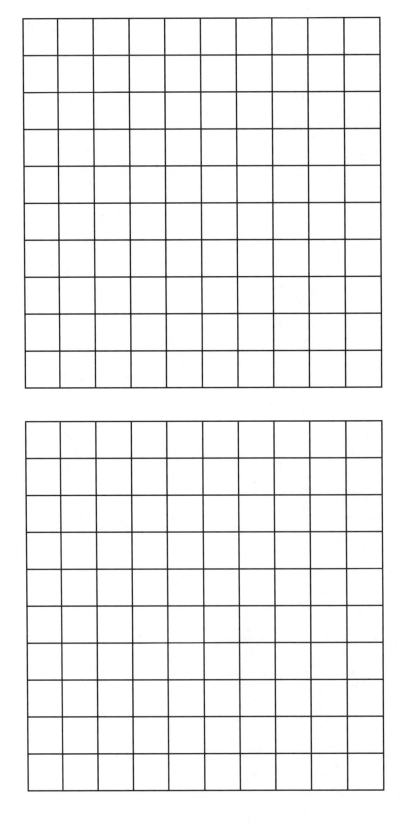

Fraction Strips

One Whole

$\frac{1}{2}$	$\frac{1}{2}$

$\frac{1}{3}$	$\frac{1}{3}$	$\frac{1}{3}$

$\frac{1}{4}$	$\frac{1}{4}$	$\frac{1}{4}$	$\frac{1}{4}$

$\frac{1}{5}$	$\frac{1}{5}$	$\frac{1}{5}$	$\frac{1}{5}$	$\frac{1}{5}$

$\frac{1}{6}$	$\frac{1}{6}$	$\frac{1}{6}$	$\frac{1}{6}$	$\frac{1}{6}$	$\frac{1}{6}$

$\frac{1}{8}$	$\frac{1}{8}$	$\frac{1}{8}$	$\frac{1}{8}$	$\frac{1}{8}$	$\frac{1}{8}$	$\frac{1}{8}$	$\frac{1}{8}$

$\frac{1}{10}$	$\frac{1}{10}$	$\frac{1}{10}$	$\frac{1}{10}$	$\frac{1}{10}$	$\frac{1}{10}$	$\frac{1}{10}$	$\frac{1}{10}$	$\frac{1}{10}$	$\frac{1}{10}$

$\frac{1}{12}$	$\frac{1}{12}$	$\frac{1}{12}$	$\frac{1}{12}$	$\frac{1}{12}$	$\frac{1}{12}$	$\frac{1}{12}$	$\frac{1}{12}$	$\frac{1}{12}$	$\frac{1}{12}$	$\frac{1}{12}$	$\frac{1}{12}$

Rulers

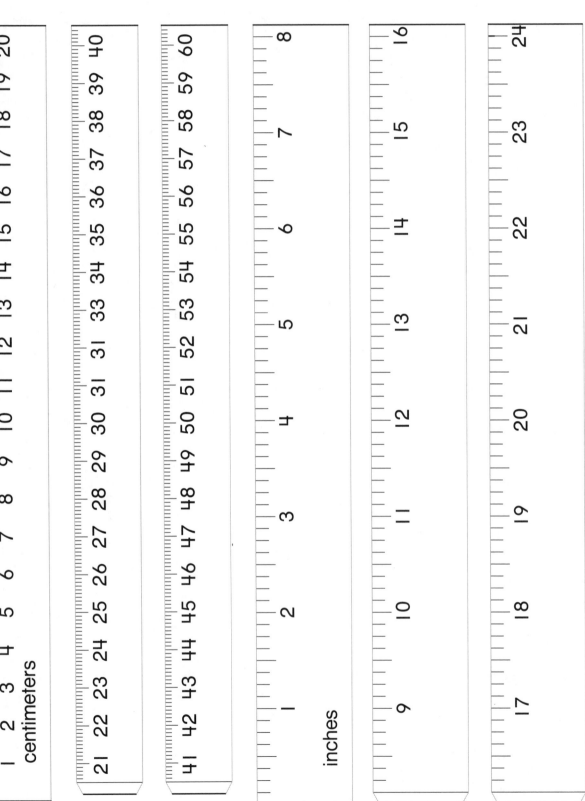

centimeters

inches

Thermometer

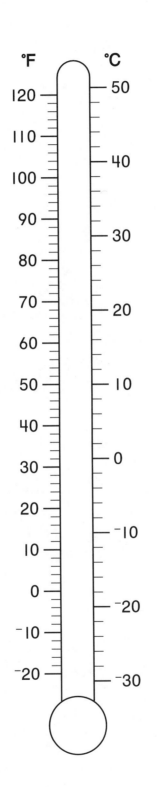

Clock Face

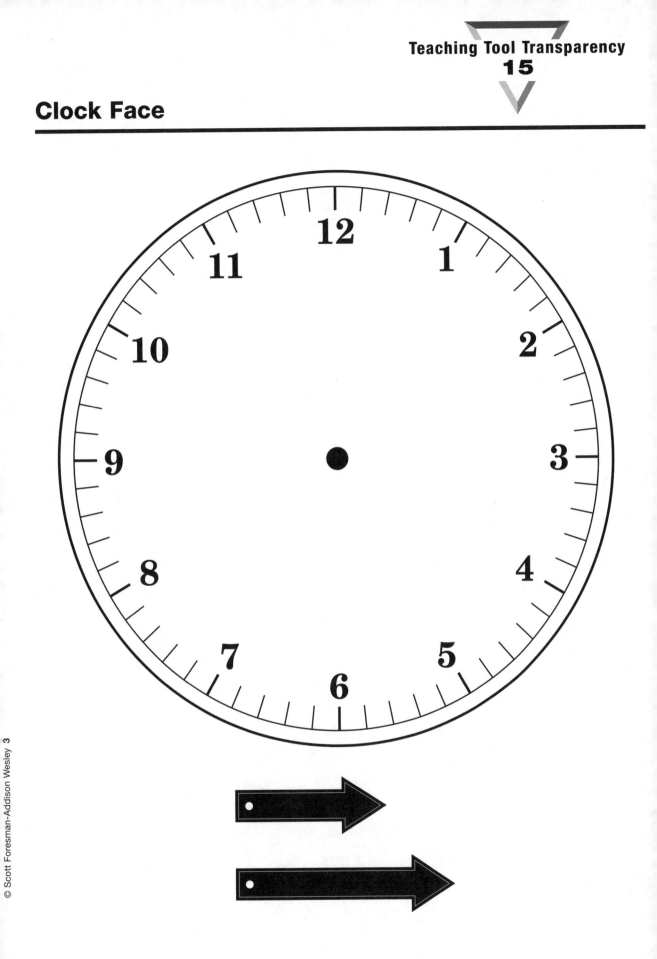

Power Polygons

Place-Value Models

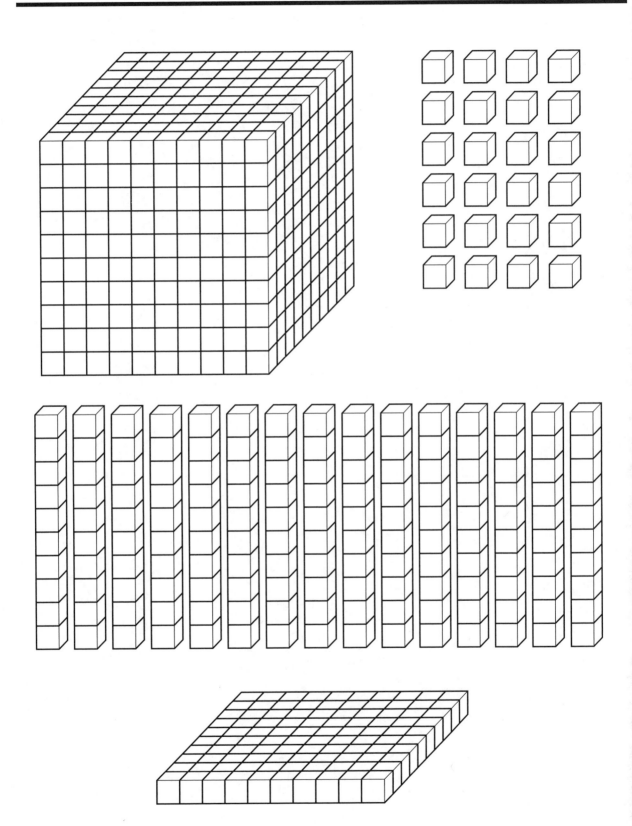

Triangle Grid Paper

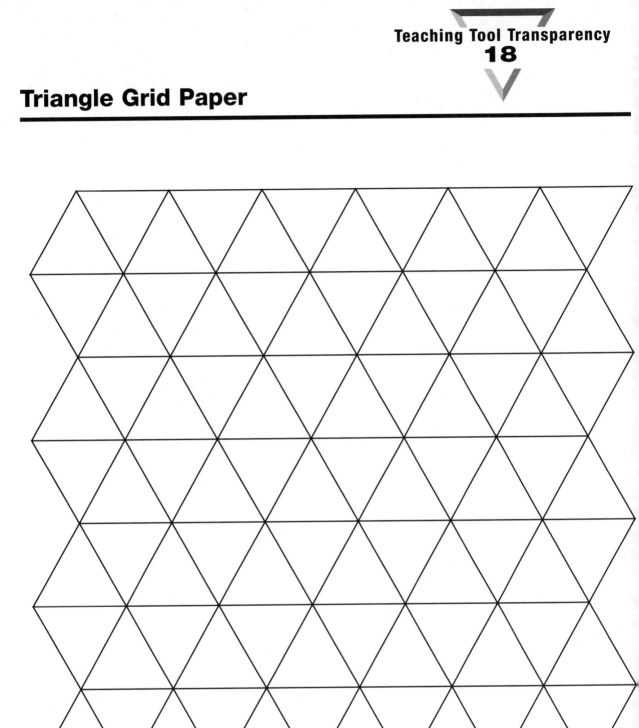

Spinners (Blanks and Halves)

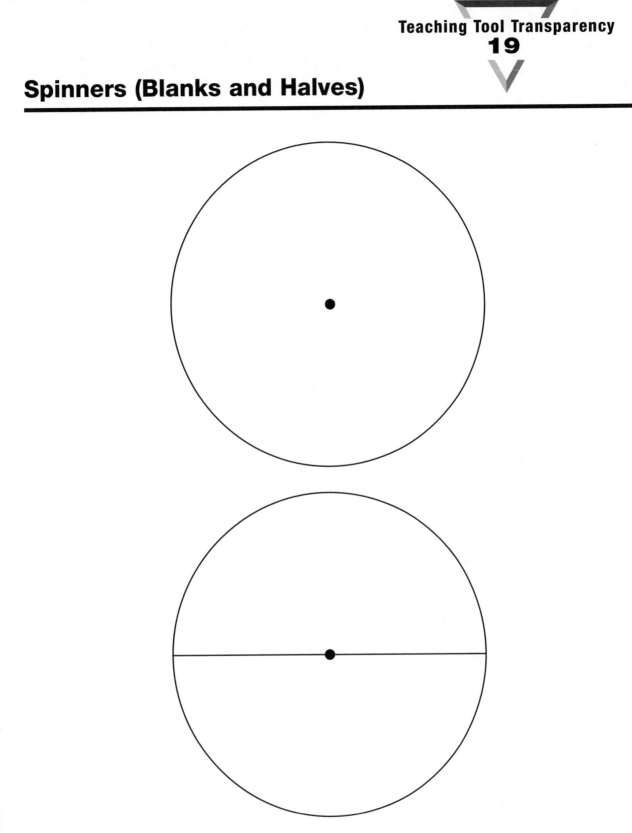

To use the spinner, place a paper clip in the center of the
circle. Then hold the pencil vertically inside the paper clip,
with the point on the center of the spinner. Keeping the pencil
in place, spin the paper clip.

Spinners (Thirds and Quarters)

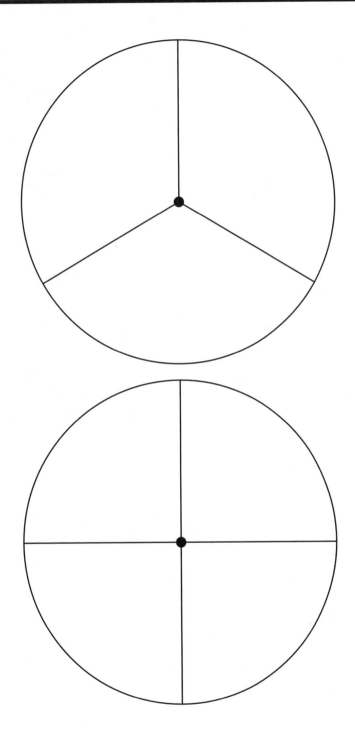

To use the spinner, place a paper clip in the center of the circle. Then hold the pencil vertically inside the paper clip, with the point on the center of the spinner. Keeping the pencil in place, spin the paper clip.

Money–Coins

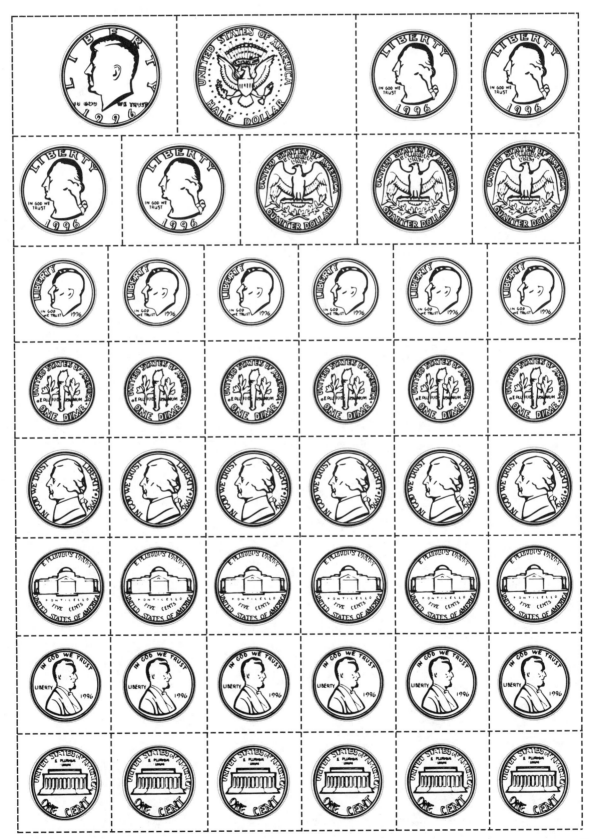

Money–Bills

Map of the United States

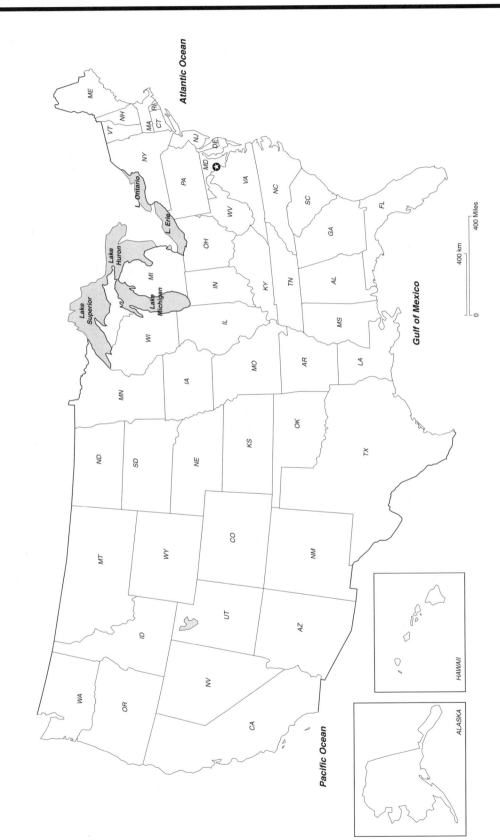

Calculator